GOD

GOD

poetry by

J. R. Solonche

SHANTI ARTS PUBLISHING
BRUNSWICK, MAINE

GOD

Published by Shanti Arts Publishing

Designed by Shanti Arts Designs

Cover image: IgorZh / istockphoto.com

Shanti Arts LLC
193 Hillside Road
Brunswick, Maine 04011
shantiarts.com

Printed in the United States of America

ISBN: 978-1-962082-10-5 (softcover)

Library of Congress Control Number: 2024932876

OTHER TITLES BY J. R. SOLONCHE

The Architect's House
The Eglantine
Alone
The Book of a Small Fisherman
The Dreams of the Gods
Around Here
The Lost Notebook of Zhao Li
The Five Notebooks of Zhao Li
Life-Size
Coming To
Selected Poems 2002–2021
Years Later
The Dust
A Guide of the Perplexed
The Moon Is the Capital of the World
For All I Know
The Time of Your Life
Enjoy Yourself
Piano Music
The Porch Poems
The Jewish Dancing Master
In a Public Place
If You Should See Me Walking on the Road
To Say the Least
True Enough
In Short Order

Tomorrow, Today, and Yesterday

Invisible

Won't Be Long

I, Emily Dickinson & Other Found Poems

Heart's Content

The Black Birch

Beautiful Day

Peach Girl: Poems for a Chinese Daughter
     (with Joan I. Siegel)

CONTENTS

PART I

QUEEN ANNE'S LACE

It is also known as wild carrot,
but the result is the same.
"Watch this, Doreen," I shouted
to my high school sweetheart
as I pulled up and scoffed down
a handful. "Don't do that. You'll
be good and sick," she shouted
back. "No, I won't. They're good
for you. They're carrots. Lots
of vitamin A," I said. Doreen was
right. I got good and sick. Doreen
was always right. After all, she
married Jeff, the quarterback.

YOU MUST ADMIRE

You must admire
how tenacious they are,
the purple petunias
as they cascade over
the planter's edge,
licking the last drop
of sun from its chin.

SUMMER

The birds don't seem
to mind the noise
my neighbor thinks
is music as they go on
minding their own summer.

I ASKED HIM

I asked him,
but he said
he didn't know
the first thing
about it, and
that really is
bad because
the first thing
is all there ever
is to know about it.

POEM FOR M.

M., you didn't need to ask.
I would have done it anyway
or instead—a very easy task—
simply quote Byron and say,
"She walks in beauty like the night
Of cloudless climes and starry skies,
And all that's best of dark and bright
Meet in her aspect and her eyes."
Ann Beatrix Wilmot was another's wife,
like you, but how could I ever do justice
to your smile, your sexy ponytail, your laugh,
your eyes, lustrous and deep, your ass?
(Yes, I really did say that!)
And I've really written you a sonnet.

TWENTY POEMS BASED ON FIRST LINES BY EMILY DICKINSON

1

Portraits are to daily faces
as poems are to daily speech.
They both live in the narrowest places,
the hardest for us to reach.

2

The me that walks and works must die.
So, too, must every other me.
Thus every single one of us shall be why
we'll make a merry company.

3

This dirty little heart
keeps dirty little secrets deep within.
Oh, how such a little body part
can hold a wilderness of sin.

4

Time does go on.
If it could speak,
it would go on and on
like any other egomaniac.

5

Time does go on,
you know, when we do not.
It is the natural motion
of the plot to find the plot.

6

Were it to be the last,
this foolish thing I write,
I still would find it fit to cast.
You sure it isn't out of spite?

7

I bring an unaccustomed wine
to dinner at your place.
The label shows a pleasant vine,
but displeasure's on your face.

8

A shade upon the mind there passes,
and passing leaves a stain
which in death's darkest ink traces
its shape upon the brain.

9

A solemn thing it was I said,
but all of you mistook it for a joke.
All, that is, except the dead
who knew full well whereof I spoke.

10

A word dropped careless on a page
can sometimes prove the best,
the most fortuitous and the sage
of all the careful rest.

11

As we passed houses musing slow.
Oh, who is slowly musing, Emily?
Is it the "we,"
or the "houses"? I don't know.

12

I meant to have but modest needs,
but as the years have passed,
I've grown greedier. Greed's
will will always my will outlast.

13

The future never spoke
as much as the past still does.
Tomorrow is silent as smoke.
Yesterday deafens with a blaze's noise.

14

It is a lonesome glee,
one I wish that I could share,
but it is private discovery,
the perfect word from out of nowhere.

15

I went to heaven
but did not hang around for long.
Everyone was squeaky clean shaven
and sang one interminable song.

16

Experiment to me
is a worthless sort of poetry.
All I hear is breaking glass.
All I smell is rubber gloves and gas.

17

Down time's quaint stream
the hours, days, weeks flow.
With or without the dream,
I stand and watch them go.

18

Circumference thou bride of awe,
you say, so awe's the groom.
But it was late—1884.
What were you smoking up in your room?

19

Of nature I shall have enough
only when the wild black cherry dies,
when the bees in its blossoms no longer laugh,
and the breeze in its branches no longer sighs.

20

Let me not mar that perfect dream
by awakening too soon.
There are so few, too few of them,
you gods, to never grant this perfect boon.

RELIGION

There they were at the brewery,
five young women, Jehovah's
Witnesses, on a break from
proselytizing in town. "You're
drinking beer?" I said. "Yes, we
do at times. We're not Mormons,
you know," one said. She was
the prettiest, the tallest, the only
one wearing a skirt, not a dress,
and the skirt was slit halfway up
the leg. I guess she was the one
assigned to convert all the men.
She should have started with me.

BIRTHDAY GIFT

My daughter bought a
tee shirt for my birthday.
It says, Badass Poet.
The first person who saw
it, a woman at the bar,
said that a tee shirt should
be a tease, a conversation-
starter and not give away
everything about the person
wearing it. "So does mine do
that, say everything about me?"
I said. "Yes, it does," she said.
"So that means I should cross
out Badass?" I said. "No,
cross out Poet," she said.

HALF A SUMMER

Half a summer
is half a golden loaf
with half a pat of butter
to be eaten with half ice,
half whiskey, half water.

WELL, AMMONS, SOMEONE

Well, Ammons, someone
wanted to know who you are,
a librarian, no less, wanted
to know who you are, but why
should I be surprised? There
are librarians, and then there
are librarians.

WHOEVER SAID HAPPINESS

Whoever said happiness
is its own punishment
knew more about
happiness than was good
for him. Either that or
more about punishment.

SECOND OF ALL, ALFRED

Second of all, Alfred,
I wanted to be a poet,
like you, more like you
than like you, less
like me than like me.

PEACE

It didn't last long. It never
does. One generation
is the most it ever does,
given man's attention span.
The next one, you'll be glad
to hear, Alfred, is shining its
boots, sharpening its bayonet,
cleaning and sighting its gun.

GREETING CARD

"You are the enemy,"
  says my brother.
"You and your liberal
  friends are the enemy
  of America," says
  my brother. "And by
  the way, Happy Birthday,"
  says my brother.

IN THE HARDWARE STORE

I went into Brett's True Value,
not because I needed anything
but I just needed to kill some
time. Besides I like walking
around hardware stores. I like
looking at stuff, and I like the
smell of hardware. I actually
found something to buy, a can
of spray dry lubricant. I love
the oxymoron of it—spray dry
lubricant. Anyway, I asked the
young lady at the register if she
liked poetry. She had bleached
hair—half bleached hair—half
no hair—heavy black stuff around
the eyes—a lot of piercings, so
I knew she would say yes. "Yes,
I love poetry. I write poetry," she
said. I knew she would say that.
I gave her a copy of *Coming To*,
which I carry around with me.
"I'd like to see your poems," I said.
"Here's my email address." "Okay,"
she said. "Do you want justice
or mercy?" I said. "I don't know.
What's the difference?" she said.
"Well, never mind," I said. "Just
keep writing." I'm sure she is.

LOVE POEM

If he hadn't done
it, I would have.
"She stands in beauty,"
I would have said.
"Her light blonde hair done
up, her eyes blue for the love
of blue, her lips, beguiling,
blushed in softest red,
and her body, the whole of it, smiling."

DID YOU EVER WRITE

Did you ever write
a love poem, Alfred?
No, I don't think you
ever did, unless they
were all silver love poems
to the silver world. And
they were all silver love
poems to the silver world.

THE COMPLAINT

Too conscious of self.
No, that's not right. Not
quite. Too self-conscious
of self is the complaint
not put right put right.

MOONBURST

It was wan.
It was white.
It was sickly white.
It was filled to full with white.
It was white as a sheet.
It saw a ghost.
It saw me.
I was the ghost it saw.
I was at the window and it saw me.
I wasn't dead but I was a ghost.
I was the ghost of the me I was this morning.
The sun saw me then.
It burst through the window.
It laughed in my face.

I WISH I KNEW MORE PEOPLE

I wish I knew more people,
interesting people,
interesting people to inspire me,
the kind of interesting people you knew, Bill,
to inspire me the way they inspired you.

THE HAPPINESS OF PURSUIT

On Monday, I pursued the gold of the sun.
On Tuesday, I pursued the silver of the moon.
On Wednesday, I pursued the platinum of the stars.
On Thursday, I pursued the crystals of salt.
On Friday, I pursued the coins of the realm.
On Saturday, I pursued a poem through the woods.
On Sunday, I pursued the widow of the dead future.

WE PLANTED NOTHING

We planted nothing
in the big boxes
on the shady side
of the house, yet here
they are, full of growth,
content to be flowerless
vicariously in the sun.

DELUSIONAL

"What reason is there
to not go on forever?"
laugh the petunias as
they go on forever
toward the sun, which
hasn't the heart to answer.

I ALWAYS WANTED TO WEAR

I always wanted to wear
a red carnation,
so I could tell her how she
would know it's me under
the clock at Grand Central Station.
Or a white one.

ON THE SONG OF WINGS

On the song of wings,
we fly over the day.

Everything sings.
We have nothing to say.

On the song of wings,
we go far, far away

where everything rings
in its own pure way.

On the song of wings,
we fly over the night.

Every star brings
us its own true light.

On the song of wings,
there is one, not two things.

PART II

GOD

When we were across the street,
me at one in the carriage and my
mother, leaning against the wall,
the white granite wall of the
Catholic church gleaming in the
bright sun of that second summer,
her hand on the handle of the carriage
thinking I was asleep in the sun,
who would have thought I, at one,
could ever remember how white
that wall was and how golden it was
across the street, against the Catholic
church where God surely, surely must
have lived, and whose hand must surely,
surely have held the handle of my carriage
next to the hand of my mother, his wife.

ANCIENT IRANIAN BRONZE

We know it was supposed to be
an honor, in fact, the greatest
honor we horses of Luristan
could have bestowed on us, but
shit, the damn thing weighed a ton.
They rubbed our glossy cheeks raw.
Nevertheless, we deigned to grin
and bear it, for weren't we famous,
we Niseans, the most prized mounts
of the Spartans and the ones who took,
in our chariots, the Persian kings to war?

WHEN THE LEAF

When the leaf
from the tree behind
me fell beside me,
I thought it was
a butterfly dying,
which is something
I have never seen
and hope never to
see unless it is like
a leaf falling gently,
gently beside me.

I WISH I HAD AN EX-WIFE

I wish I had an ex-wife.
Ex-wives are so much more
interesting than wives,
so much more exciting, so
much sexier. I wish I had
an ex-wife who would call
me and ask, "Are you busy?
Have you written yet? May
I come over?" I wish I had
an ex-wife who would come
over when I'm not busy,
after I have written enough
for the day, when I'm just
having my last drink. The ex-
wives of poets are the best.
There are so many of them.
And they're the sexiest.

UNTITLED

"Steel silence hangs in the balance
  That those are a man's dime-like thoughts,"
  is what you said, Alfred,
  increasing tenfold the worth of thoughts.
  What would you call that?
  I would call that generosity of spirit.
  I would call that goodness of heart.
  I would call that a poet's innocent foolishness.
  What you would call a poet's foolish innocence.

SHORTCUTS

"Remember, there are no shortcuts,"
he used to say. He was my father,
and he used to say that a lot. I think
he said that more than he said anything.
I knew what he meant. He didn't need
to spell it out. So, of course, I took all
the shortcuts I could find. The shortcut
to the ball field. The shortcut to the
candy store. The shortcut to the deli.
The shortcut to the pizza place. The
shortcut to the junior high school.
The shortcut to the high school. The
shortcut to the B average in high
school. The shortcut to the college
across town. The shortcut to dropping
out. The shortcut to the woman I
married. The shortcut to becoming
a poet. I never told him he was right.

OF WHAT

It's most of the calls now.
The news of the deaths.
Of the colleagues. Of the
friends. Of the neighbors.
Of those we barely knew
but will remember when
reminded. "Oh, yes, wasn't
he the one who . . . ?" we say.
"Was it a heart attack? Was
it cancer? Cancer of what?"
we say. "Of the bladder? Of
the prostate? Of the throat?
Of the stomach?" we say.
And why do we need to
know? Why the fuck do we
need to know of what? Can't
we just know he died? Isn't
that enough? Oh, no. That
isn't enough. We do. Yes,
we do need to know of what.

THE NUMBER OF BOOKS

The shelf knows the right number of books.
The shelf laughs as it gets lighter.
The shelf welcomes the light with open arms.
The shelf makes the case for the light number of books.
The shelf makes the case for itself.
The shelf shelves the question indefinitely.

SONG OF THE MIRACLE

The miracle happened while you were away.
What a shame you weren't there.
Of course, it would have happened anyway.
Of course, the miracle didn't care
that it was a miracle you missed.
It happened because it saw itself in the glass.
The miracle fell in love with its image. They kissed.
One was sublime, the other ridiculous.

THE FLAG

It has stripes.
It has red stripes.
It has white stripes.
It has stars.
Of stars, there are fifty.
They twinkle on a field of blue.
It is fastened to the poles of my neighbors.
It hangs there all day and all night in all weather.
It is a grand old flag.
It is a high flying flag.
It is a flag that covers a multitude of sins.
It is a flag that covers the sins of multitudes.

THE ORCHARD

Not many people at the orchard,
but we all buy corn, bicolor and
very sweet. "Where are the peaches?"
someone asks. "Sold out last week," she
answers. "A bad year for peaches?" he
says. "Yes, bad for peaches but a good
year for other things," she says. "Like
corn, I see," he says. "Yes, and other
things, too," she says, pointing to other
things. "Isn't every year like that, though?
Good for some things but not for others?"
he asks. "Yes, like people. Good for some
but not for others," she says. They nod in
agreement. They laugh. There is nothing
worse than the philosophy of the orchard.

CONCERT

Once, twice, the conductor
gave the down beat, but
the chorus, first once, then
twice was late, so for a third
time she began, and all now
kept the music steady until
the last chord, which she
called for longer than the
score called for, twice as long.

WISDOM

It is the shadow
that knows the most
about the sun.

PAYOFF

A white butterfly has
wakened another asleep
or pretending to sleep,
and more persistent than I
have ever been with my
wife, it was rewarded
with a kiss of wings.

BAD HABITS

I quit smoking years ago,
but sometimes I pick up
my pen, put it in my mouth,
and try to light it with my
thumb. Will the same thing
happen when I quit writing?

AT THE WINDOW

Too many roads
in the world.

Too many cars
in the world.

Too much world
in the world.

MY UNKNOWN DISCIPLE

Too brash?
Why too?
Is brash alone too thin a brush?
There must be one disciple.
Why not?
There has to be.
Anyway, I claim him on principle.

HAIRCUT

"He was the best president
in our history," I heard him
say, the elderly man I thought
was talking about Lincoln, or
Washington, or FDR. As a boy,
he could have remembered FDR.
He could have heard him on the
radio giving a Fireside Chat. He
could have remembered the funeral
train. But when he said, "He's a
self-made millionaire," I knew
he was talking about Trump, and
all I wanted to do was grab a towel
and shove it down his throat. Shit,
I wish I had. I've always wanted
to write a poem sitting in jail.

I WISH I WERE BACK IN SCHOOL

I wish I were back in school.
I wish I were sitting in class
again at my desk behind the
girl with the long blonde braid.
I don't remember her name.
I remember that whenever she
caught me looking at her, she
smiled and looked away. This
time I will say what I wanted
to say back then but was afraid.
"You have the most beautiful
hair in the world," I will say.
Then I will tell her to tie it
around my neck in a golden
leash and lead me around as
if I were her prisoner and slave,
for I would be her prisoner and
slave forever and ever. I wish
I were back in school to be the
fool of love she would remember,
they would all remember, forever.

COLOR

The scientists say it doesn't exist.
Tell that to the bees.
Tell that to the butterflies.
Tell that to the birds-of-paradise.
Tell that to Mark Rothko.

I HAD ROSES

I had roses.
I have no roses now.
I did not take care of my roses.
My roses were red.
My roses looked spectacular by the yellow lilies.
My roses looked spectacular by the front door.
Of my roses visitors would say, "Your roses look
        spectacular."
This was years ago.
This was about the time my wife got sick.

WISHING WELL

My neighbor has one
in his yard, a wishing
well. I have never seen
him make a wish there.
I have never seen his
daughters make a wish
there. I have never seen
his wife make a wish there,
but I have seen her in the
evening in the bathroom
window brushing her hair,
the look of wishing well
on her face.

I FORGOT THEY ARE FLOWERS

I've been looking
at them for so long,
for nearly half a year,
I forgot they are flowers,
the petunias, pink and
purple, the marigolds,
yellow and orange, but
this is of no consequence,
for the bees remembered.

DEMENTIA

Her left hand is a claw
so tightly clenched it
takes one of us to unfold
the fingers, the other to cut
the nails, useless unless
she holds the memories
there, but with the right
she eats, and in bed, at
night or in the afternoon,
asleep or awake or between,
she plays Bach or Chopin or
something never known before
and never to be known again.

WHEN I AM CONFRONTED

When I am confronted by a flower,
any flower, a rose, a daisy, a lily,
a petunia, it doesn't matter,
I pray for the usefulness of a bee,
for all I am able to do is stare uselessly.

AFTER THE READING

After the reading, a woman
came up to me and said, "You
really are a sentimental son-
of-a-bitch, aren't you?" "What
makes you say that?" I asked.
"You write about your cats only
when they die," she said.

USE

"Make yourself useful," my
mother would say as she tossed
me a dish towel, or a garbage
bag, or the broom when I was
a kid. So I did. I made myself
useful. I dried the dishes with
the towel. I bagged the garbage
with the garbage bag. I swept
the porch with the broom. That
was when I thought about the
most useless future I could think
of for myself. That was when
I first thought of being a minor
nobleman of a very small country
in central Europe. Or a poet.

HAPPIEST MOMENT

My friend, Jim, gave me *The
Collected Stories of Lydia
Davis*. I never heard of Lydia
Davis, so I'm glad he gave me
the book because I really like
her stories, especially the very
short ones which are actually
prose poems and which remind
me of me. I think my favorite
story is "Kafka Cooks Dinner,"
probably because I'm Jewish
like Kafka, and like him, I, too,
don't know what that means.
Another favorite is "Happiest
Moment." It made me think of
my happiest moment, which is
what any reader would, of course,
want to think of. It should have
been easy, but it wasn't because
I'm still thinking. It could be the
moment I wrote the last line of
my one and only sestina. Or it
could be the moment I opened
the birthday present and found
the Red Ryder Daisy BB gun
I always wanted. Or it could be
the moment I ejaculated on my

wife's ass before she was my wife.
Or it could be the moment I was
Zeed out of the army, which meant
I wouldn't be going to Vietnam.
Now that I think of it, I think that
was my happiest moment, for I
whistled the whole way back to
the Bronx from Whitehall Street
on the subway. Or maybe it was
the moment I learned to whistle.

LINDSAY

Her name is Lindsay. She
works in the Greek restaurant.
She doesn't look Greek, but
she could be. She has a lot of
tattoos. I don't like women with
a lot of tattoos. Tattoos ruin their
beautiful shoulders and arms.
They ought to be more discreet.
One or two small ones on the ankle
or the wrist. But when she said she
had a line from Bukowski tattooed
on her back, I forgave her the others.

WHAT WE KNEW

We knew some things.
Most were not worth knowing.
But we did not know until it was too late.
Isn't that just like us?

THE HUMMINGBIRDS ARE GONE

The last one left yesterday.
Godspeed, hummingbirds.

May you arrive safe and sound in Mexico.
Buena suerte, colibríes.

Que llegues sano y salvo a México.
Viva!

Viva, colibries!
Que regresen el próximo año, hermanos y
hermanas!

I WAS ATTRACTED

I was attracted to an attractive
woman fixing herself a cup of
coffee in the supermarket. She
was tall. She was blonde. She
had a great body for a woman
in her fifties or possibly sixties.
I was attracted and wanted to
go over to the coffee bar next
to her and say, "What's a girl
like you doing in a place like this?"
I wanted her to say, "Fresh,"and
slap me in the face. I've always
wanted an attractive woman to do
that. Well, not always. Only lately.

POEM

(With apologies to Lydia Davis)

"First a poet writes a story about a mouse, in moonlight
in the snow,
how the mouse tries to hide in his shadow, how the
mouse climbs
up his sleeve and he shakes it down into the snow
before he knows
what it is that is clinging to his sleeve. His cat is
nearby and her
shadow is on the snow, and she is after the mouse."

We are never told the end of the story, and that's
because it is a poet who writes
it, not a writer of stories. And because it is a poet who
writes the
story, the mouse is not a mouse but a metaphor. The
mouse is the
poet. The cat is not a cat but a metaphor. The cat is
the Angel of
Death. The sleeve, however, is not a metaphor. The
sleeve is a
sleeve. The arm is a metaphor. Anyway, the moral is
do not expect
an ending in a story by a poet.

REUNITED

When the rain stopped,
the wind, unburdened,
came on so forcefully it
lifted the fallen ash leaves
back again into the waiting
arms of the ash tree.

JUST AS YESTERDAY

Just as yesterday,
the wind continues
to loosen the leaves
and then lift them
aloft again in one
upsweep almost as
far as where they
began, so familiar
it makes me wonder
if there ever was a
yesterday at all.

DEATH WISH

A butterfly was lingering
around these clusters
of flowers, small, white
flowers atop slender stalks,
for so long, I began to think
it wished to die upon them.
I would if I were a butterfly.
Or not a butterfly.

WHAT ALL POETS SHOULD KNOW

All poets should know the first poem they ever wrote by heart.
All poets should know a hawk from a handsaw.
All poets should know what their names mean.
All poets should know Susie like I knew Susie.
All poets should know their worth in salt.
All poets should know seven words that rhyme with womb.
All poets should know at least one poem by Emily Dickinson
        other than "I never saw a Moor" by heart.
All poets should know at least one poem
        by William Carlos Williams
other than "The Red Wheelbarrow" by heart.
All poets should know what a Moor looks like.
All poets should know what kind of hat Marianne Moore wore.
All poets should know what Wallace Stevens once said.
All poets should know what their name looks like
        in Chinese.
All poets should know that a poem should be read
        with one's nerves.
All poets should know William Stafford's cure
        for writer's block.
All poets should know what baseball team
        Marianne Moore rooted for.
All poets should know that the Irish bards wore
        the king's colors less one.
All poets should know that the Irish bards sat at
        the king's right hand.
All poets should know how ink is manufactured.

All poets should know how to play tennis without a net.
All poets should know how pencils are manufactured.
All poets should know how paper is manufactured.
All poets should know their cholesterol level.
All poets should know the back of their hand.
All poets should know what to do with a red wheelbarrow.
All poets should know their heart by heart.

ULYSSES

What do you know?
Blazes strung old Leo's bow.

I WOKE FROM A NAP

I woke from a nap.
I remembered a dream,
but I do not know if
it was from just now
or from last night or
from years ago. It was
so exquisitely real, it
must be from years ago.

OCEANS

Reading your "Ocean," Alfred,
makes me miss the oceans,
the two I went to and remember spreading
their "glee along the coastlines" of the east and the west.
You make me miss them, the oceans I will never go to again.

ONCE THERE WAS A CLOUD

that looked like so much like an angel,
it could have been an angel,
for it evaporated in the wind,
which is the way angels also die.

STAY OUT OF STORES

Stay out of doors
if you want to know
the seasons inside
and out. Only stay
out of stores, for
they will play with
your mind and untune
your sense of time
to have you believing
in fraudulent years.

ON BEING CHALLENGED TO WRITE A POEM ABOUT FINGERNAILS

(Well, Ken Chen has written one that starts out about
fingernails, but it ends up in a totally different place.
And Bukowski uses the word "Fingernails" in the title
of a poem but not in the poem. So here's a poem that's
all fingernails.)

The optometrist's
receptionist has long
nails, yet she is able
to perform every task
a receptionist has to do.
She answers the phone.
She uses the computer.
She writes with pen on
paper. I don't know
about the optometrist,
but I for one would not
want to have sex with
his receptionist.

THE NINE LEVELS OF NOTHING

I watched a lecture
by an astrophysicist
called "The Nine
Levels of Nothing."
I'm sure it was true,
but it was nowhere
near as much fun as
The Nine Levels of Hell.

ROADKILL

I smelled it first, three
seconds of death down
the lungs, before I saw it,
the groundhog on its back
there in the middle of the road,
meeting of careless man and
careless animal, a coincidence
of carelessness. But, oh, how
hard, how hard it is to blame
this thing on nothing more than
carelessness, than coincidence.
How hard to choke on a better
blame. How hard to be so easy.

ADAM

Yes, I was the first man.
I was not the first living
thing, though. He created
all the others before He
created me, but I was
the only one among us
to know guilt. Still am.

THE SERPENT

Ha! Ha! Losing my legs
to crawl on my belly is a
small price to pay for
the great thing I did. I can
still speak. Can you hear?
I can still laugh.

EVE

They tell me I was born
twice, the first time from
the rib of the man, the second
from the same mud as his.
I don't know which is true.
I know only that I died once.

CAIN

Adam, my father, may have
been the first man, but I,
Cain, was the first newborn,
the first toddler, the first
bratty kid. Ha! They didn't
have the faintest idea of
what to do with me. What
did they expect?

ABEL

I had the advantage of
being second. They had
experience, but Yahweh
had other plans. He always
does. Anyway, it was quick.
I didn't see it coming, that
one blow to the back of
my head. I didn't feel a thing.

LIKE THE SURPRISE

Like the surprise
of the flowering weeds,
the sound of the bees,
the season's smallest,
among them, the smallest
bees' smallest sound dying
out among them dying out,
but of them the noblest.

OCTOBER'S LIGHT IS LATE TO RISE

October's light is late to rise.
I need to stand to see it through the trees,
and even then, it is dim amid the leaves.
Soon enough it comes into its own.
It comes into its own soon enough.

OCTOBER PASTORAL

The summer wanes.
The sun does the moon's work.
The wind blames the trees.
The trees blame the wind.
The clouds ask, "What have you done?"
The shadows make sounds this year has never heard.
The chorus quiets, quits one tree frog at a time.
My beard is longer than "I haven't shaved."
The clouds have mastered gray.
A crow knows what time it is.
The only shadow is the other crow.
The tiniest wasps have the tiniest flowers to themselves.

THE WORLD

Unlike, you, Bill, I no longer
everyday walk out to my car,
but I do walk out for the sake
of walking out, for the sake
of seeing the wild black cherry
tree continue making cherry
blossoms in its mind for next
April. (Yes, it does have a mind,
a mind of its own.) I wish I could
invite the world here to walk out
with me next April to see it, for
it would do the world good to see
the wild black cherry tree in bloom.
Nonsense? Yes, that, too, would
do the world good, this sad, this
sorely bad world. It needs as much
good as it can find. It needs as much
nonsense as it can take. Then more
of both. Oh, hell, I wish just the two
of us could have walked out alone.

ABOUT THE AUTHOR

Photo: Emily Solonche

Nominated for the National Book Award, the Eric Hoffer Book Award, and nominated three times for the Pulitzer Prize, J. R. Solonche is the author of thirty-six books of poetry and coauthor of another. He lives in the Hudson Valley.

www.ingramcontent.com/pod-product-compliance
Lightning Source LLC
Chambersburg PA
CBHW071354090426
42738CB00012B/3111